Mephisto's Spree

Op. 84

by

Dr. Gregory J. Jackson

This book is presented only as a means of adding to the literature of percussion. Neither the publisher nor the author makes any representation, warranty, or guarantee that techniques or rhythms described will be effective in every musical situation or will completely make the reader a better performer without practice.

Distributed in the United States by CreateSpace, and internationally by CreateSpace. 100 Enterprise Way, Suite A200 Scotts Valley, CA 95066 USA

Printed in the United States of America

ISBN-13: 978-1499188547

ISBN-10: 1499188544

First edition, 2014
12 11 10 09 08 07 06   10 9 8 7 6 5 4 3 2

www.inner3.com

Acknowledgments

This book is dedicated to Scott Johnson and all members of the Blue Devil Drumline past, present, and future. There are many DCI groups that I loved as a kid, but the Concord Blue Devils were the most influential. Over the years I had the opportunity to know many members of the group and staff, as well as the occasional conversation with Scott. In 2004 I performed my PASIC solo in front of many of the Devs which is a moment I will remember forever. I do not know Scott extremely well, but this book is my way of thanking him and the Blue Devils for inspiring me during my early years, and even now.

Soli Deo Gloria

About the Author

Dr. Gregory Jackson is a well-recognized percussionist, composer, educator, and author. He is a multi-faceted percussion specialist in many areas. Dr. Jackson has published several books sold worldwide including 30 Timpani Etudes Op. 56, Jackson's Rudiment Dictionary, The Synergy Method for Marimba, Etudes Op. 48, The Well Tempered Marimbist Op. 46, Legendary Op. 44, Congas Full Circle, Phenom: The Excellence of Execution, and the percussion method book The Synergy Method for Drumming Vol. 1 and Vol. 2. He also has several recordings, including his 3 CDs of his compositions, two instructional percussion DVDs titled Congas Decoded and Elements of Synergy. More than 2 dozen performances of Jackson's compositions occur each year around the world. Currently, he has completed his second symphony and has more than eighty completed works. Top authorities in percussion have proclaimed that Jackson's works are filling a void in the percussion community not often addressed. Dr. Jackson performs across the country on a regular basis performing his latest works and is a member of the Percussive Arts Society Composition Committee. In the Percussive Arts Society International Collegiate Snare Competition, he placed in the top 10 four consecutive years and top 4 two years performing original solos. As an educator, he served as a consultant to three Drum Corps International Individuals Champions in 2004, 2005, and 2007 as well as the 2006 Percussive Arts Society International Competition Collegiate Champion. Jackson proudly endorses Remo Inc., Pearl Percussion, and Pro-mark sticks and mallets.

About this book

The "Shopping Spree" has been around the drumming community for decades. The name shopping spree most likely comes from the phrase "shopping for more notes". It is essentially an exercise for developing specific techniques and rudiments. The standard formula consists of alternating check patterns and various rudiments or passages. However, in the mid-90's the shopping spree evolved into a virtuosic display of a performers ability.

The world of rudimental drumming saw a shift during the 21st century and the shopping spree became slightly less of a highlight. This book is an attempt to leave a mark in the historical records so musicologists will know of the importance of this rudimental etude, and hopefully cause a rebirth of this classic. To avoid conflict, popular shopping sprees such as the Blue Devil sprees are not included in this work due to respect of copyright, but those particular exercises are available for purchase.

Most of my books are for all performance levels from beginning to advanced. For those that have never played a shopping spree, the first ones are a good start. Each etude by design becomes progressively more difficult. Initially, the stickings are provided, but the performer should keep in mind that every other measure is the check pattern which shall remain the same unless otherwise indicated. There are also a couple of bonus pieces from my first book, *The Synergy Method for Drumming Vol. 1*, that are found at the end of the book.

For any questions, feel free to contact me through the website:

www.inner3.com

If your ensemble decides to perform one of the etudes in this book, please let me know which one and I would love to see a video or hear a recording.

As a great man once said, "if you're not having fun, you are doing it wrong!"

Legend

Rim Shot

Play on the rim of the drum

One handed buzz

R

R
Right Hand

L
Left Hand

(continue until another
sticking is indicated)

B
Both Hands

Use alternating sticking unless otherwise noted. If the first note has a R displayed, begin
the exercise on the right hand but follow with a sequence of L R L etc. until another
sticking appears.

#1

G. J. Jackson

#2

G. J. Jackson

#3

G. J. Jackson

R l r R l r L r l L r l sticking for all check patterns

#4

G. J. Jackson

#5

G. J. Jackson

#6

G. J. Jackson

#7

G. J. Jackson

8

#7

9

r L r l l R l R R R R l r l r L L L L r l r l

R R R L L L R R R L L L

#8

G. J. Jackson

#9

G. J. Jackson

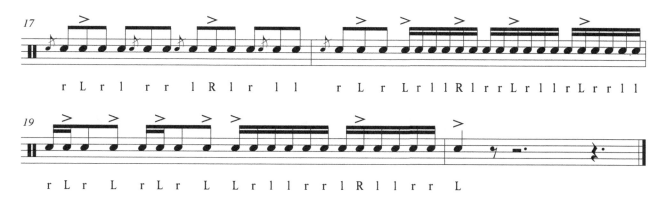

#10

G. J. Jackson

R l l L r r R l l L r r R l r r l L r l l r R l r r l L r l l r R l r r l l R l r r l l r

R l l L r r R l l L r r   R l r l l L r l r r R l r l l L r l r r

L r l l r L r l l r   r r l l r r l l r r l l R

#11

G. J. Jackson

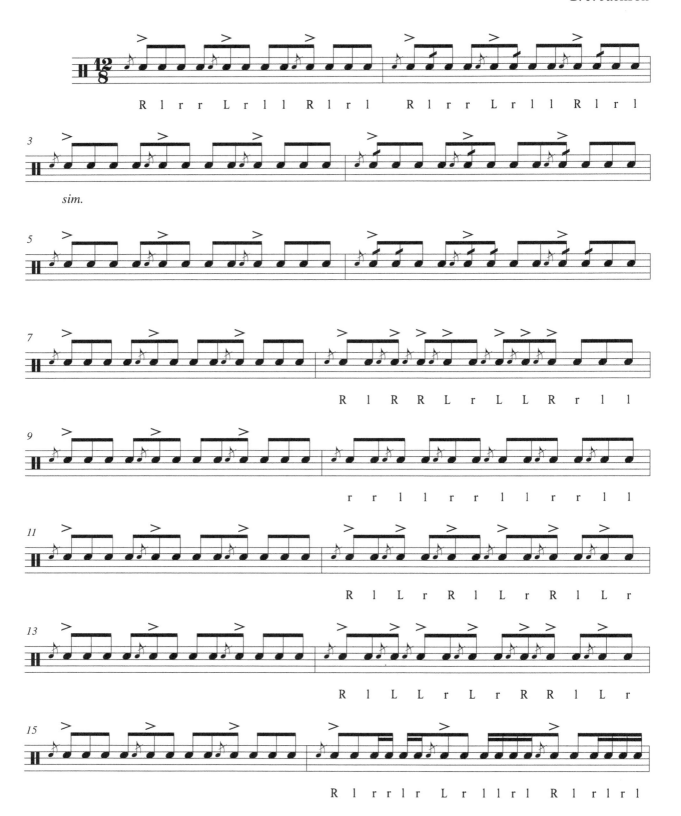

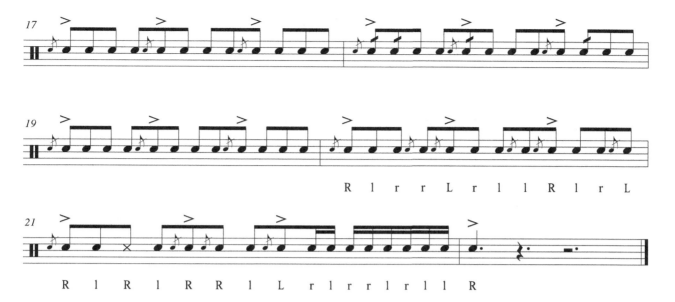

R l r r L r l l R l r L

R l R l R R l L r l r r l r l l R

#12

G. J. Jackson

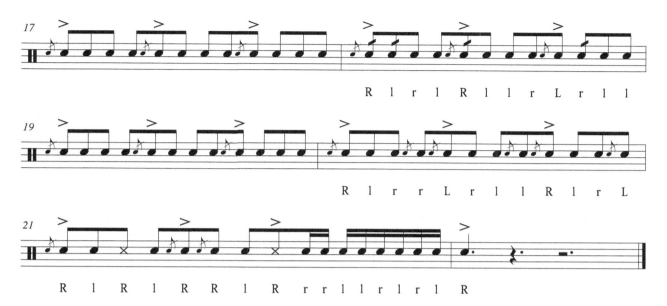

R l r l R l l r L r l l

R l r r L r l l R l r L

R l R l R R l R r r l l r l r l R

#13

G. J. Jackson

17

R l r r L r l l R l r r L r l l

19

R L R R L R L L R L R R L R L L

#14

G. J. Jackson

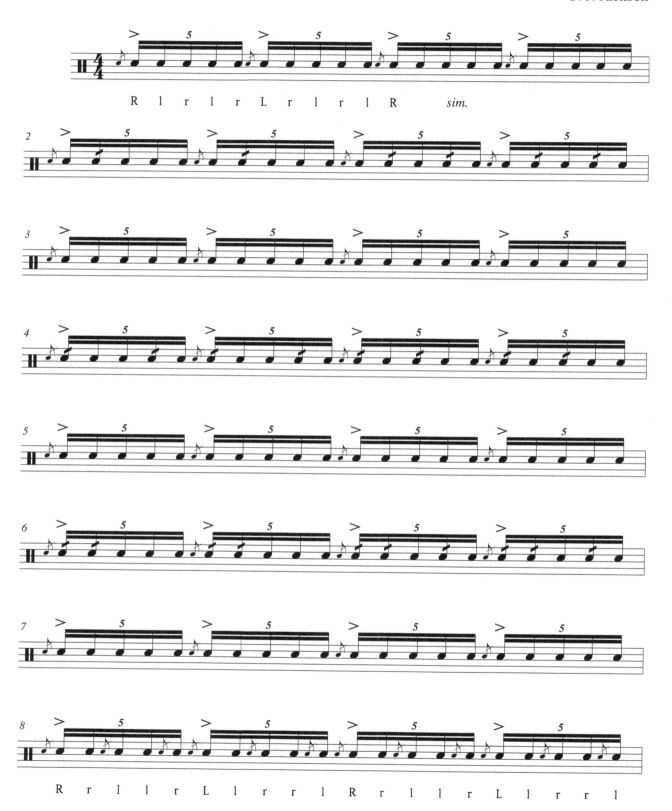

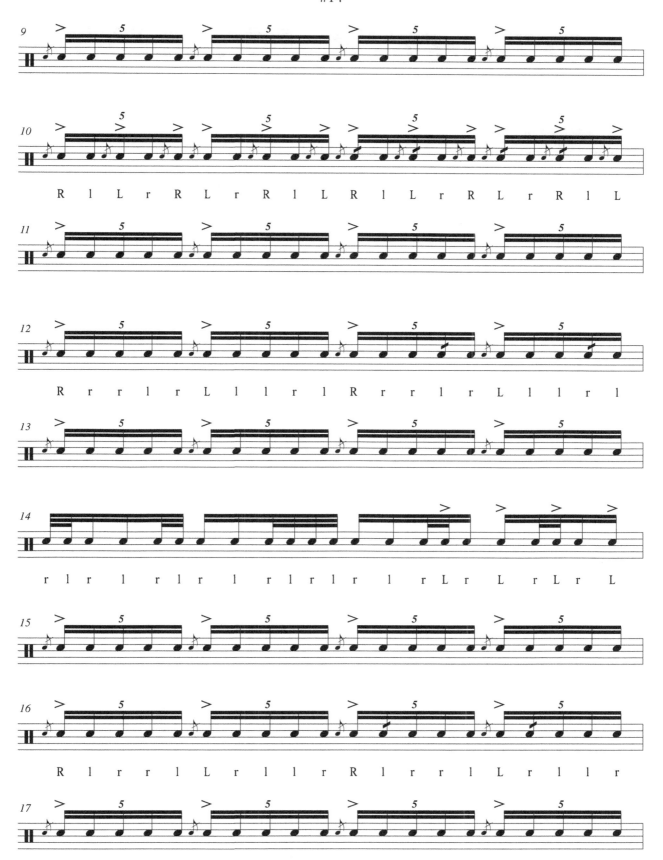

#15

G. J. Jackson

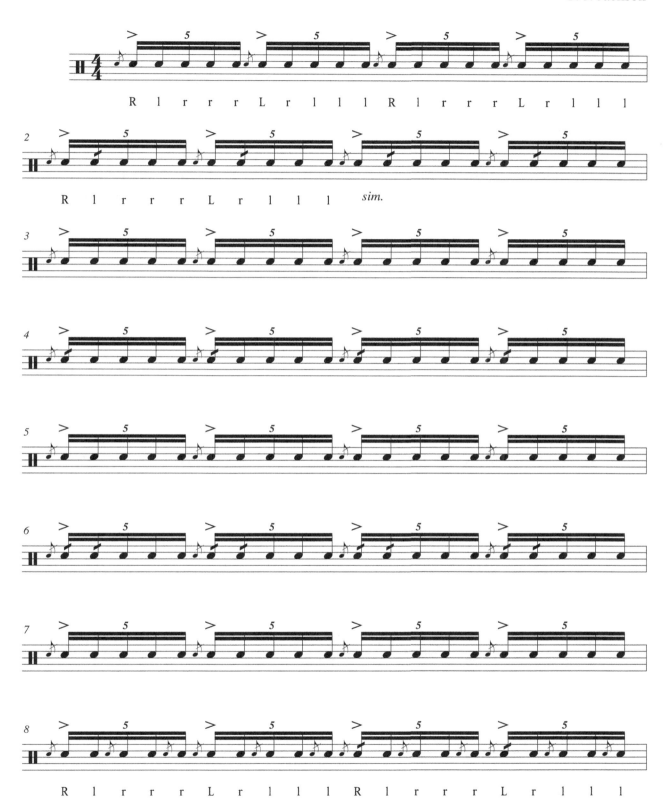

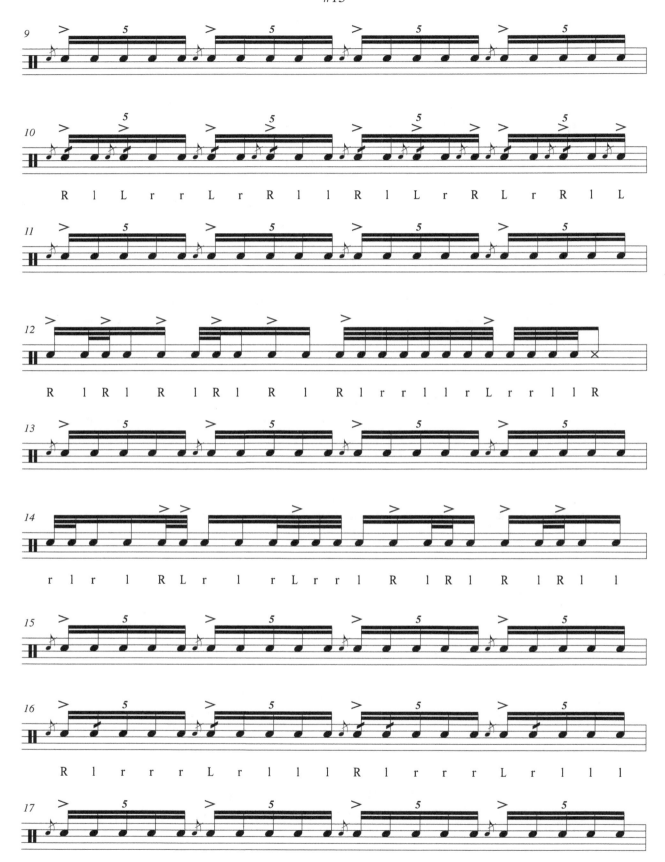

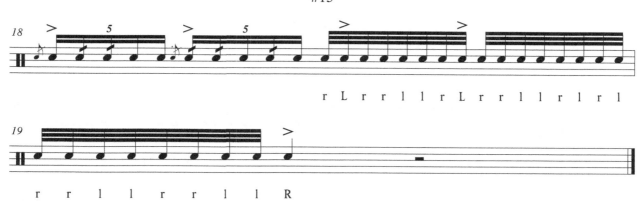

r L r r l l r L r r l l r l r l

r r l l r r l l R

#16

G. J. Jackson

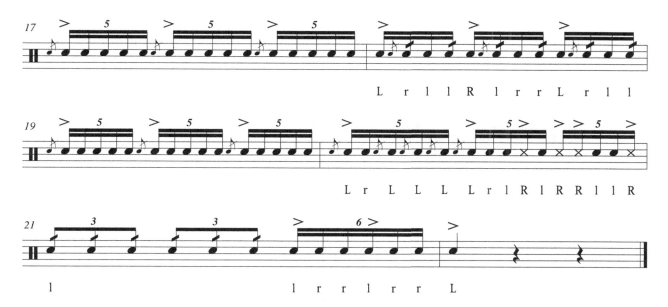

#17

G. J. Jackson

30

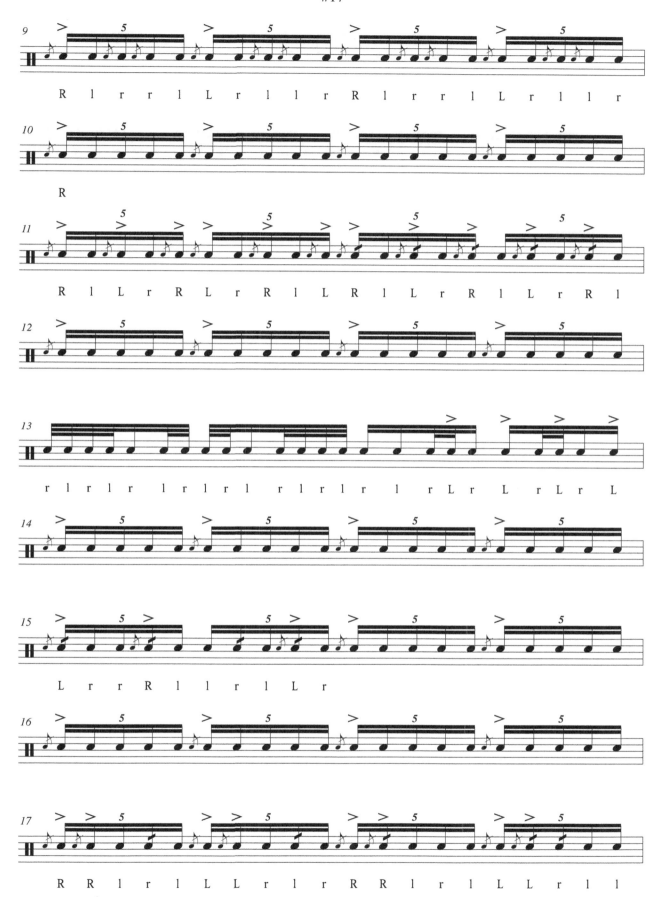

#18

G. J. Jackson

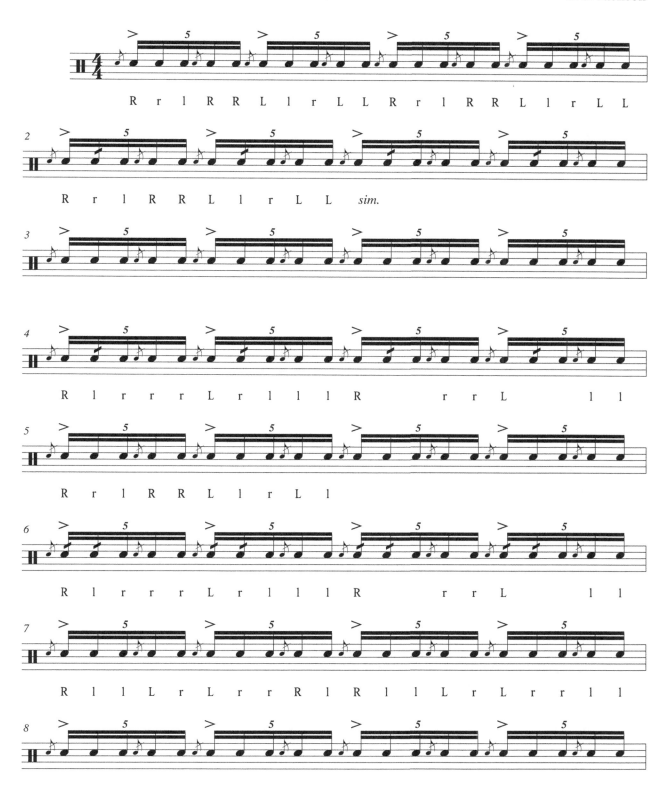

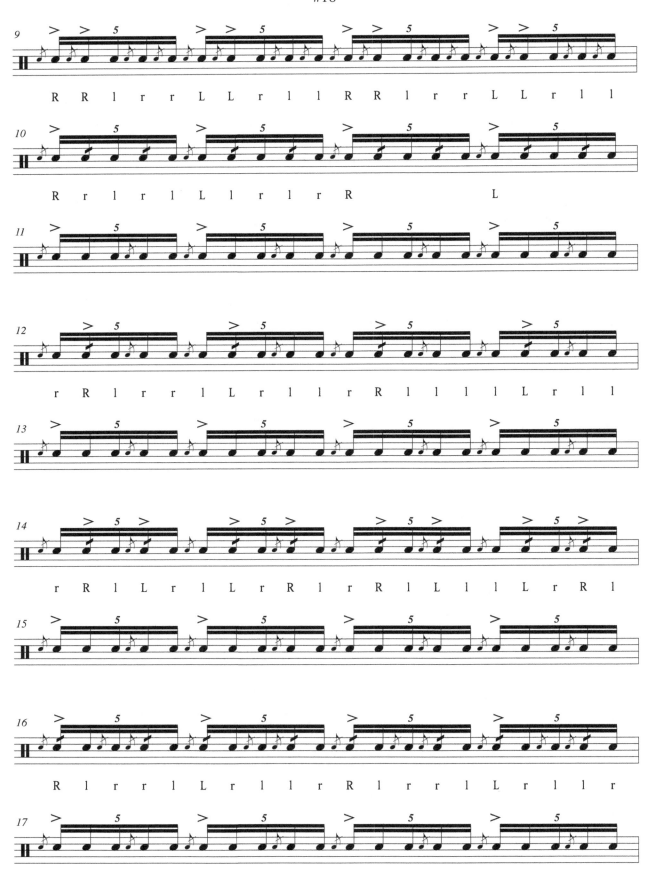

#19

G. J. Jackson

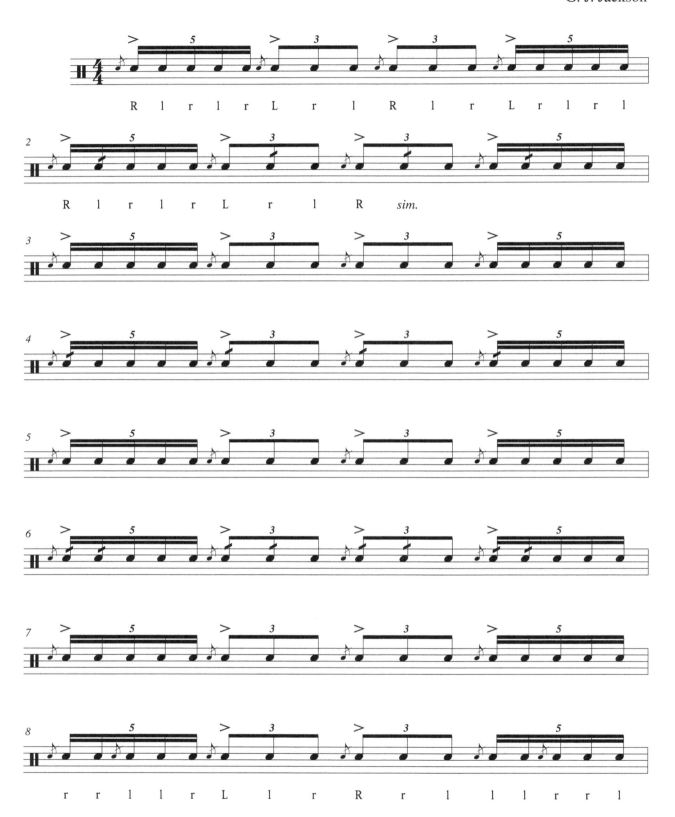

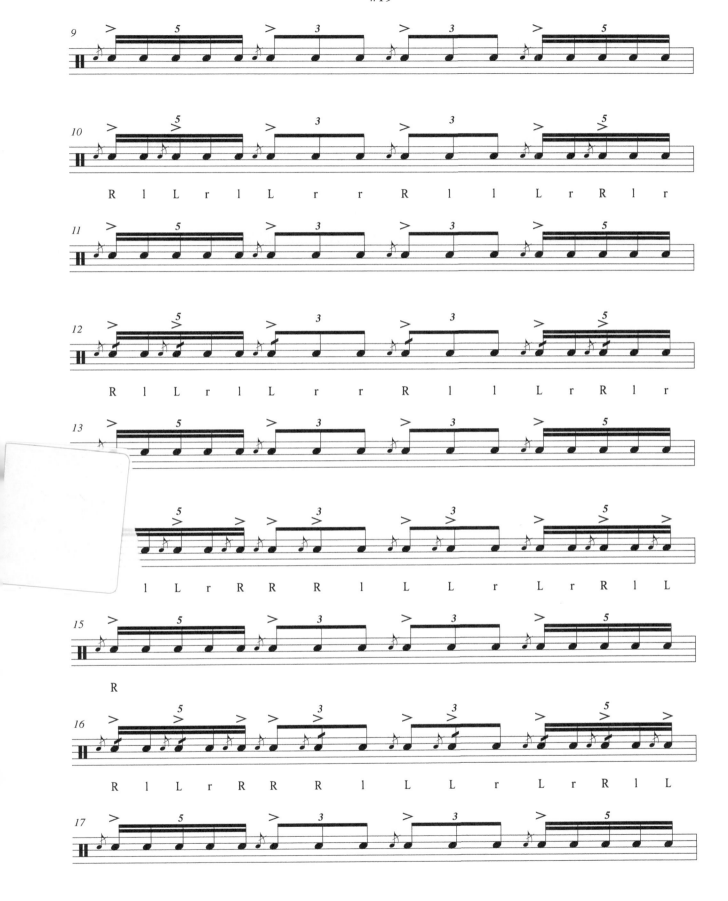

R l r l r L l r R r l L r l r l

#20

G. J. Jackson

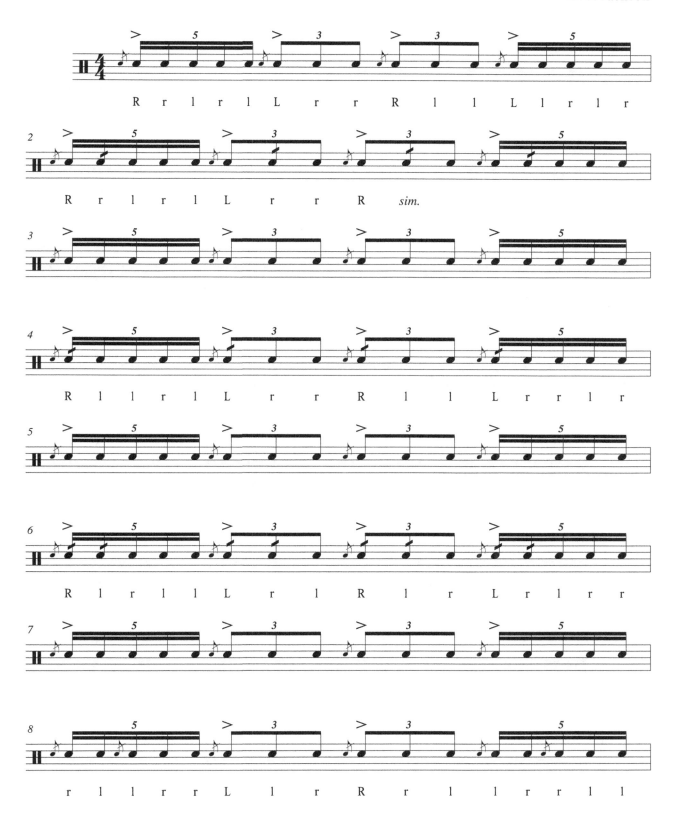

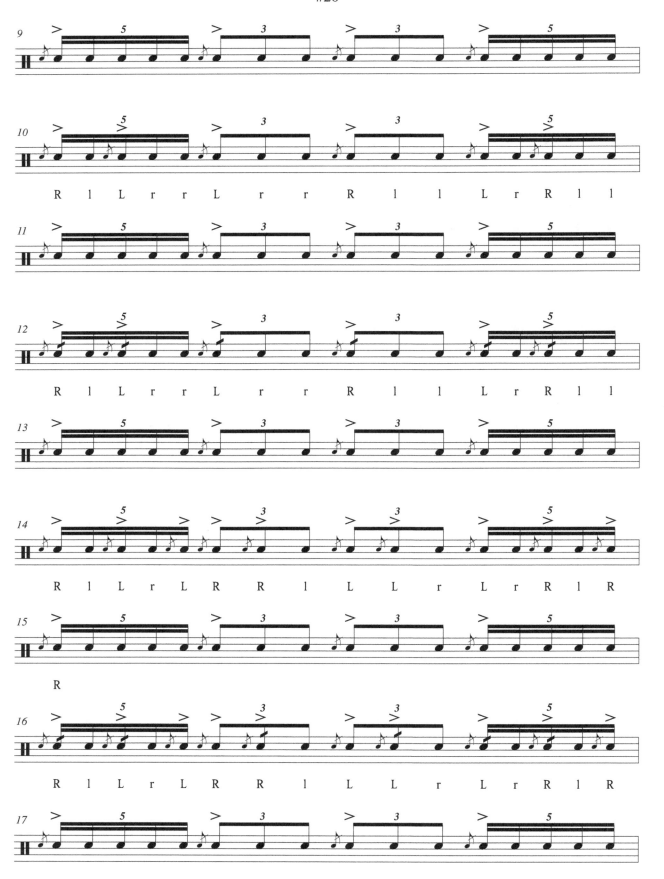

#21

G. J. Jackson

#22

G. J. Jackson

#22

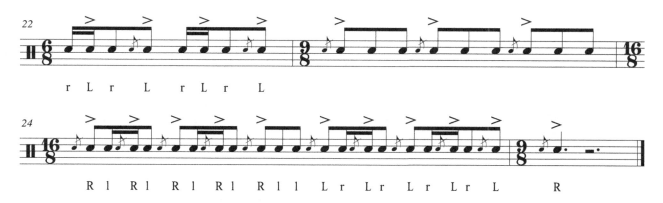

#23

G. J. Jackson

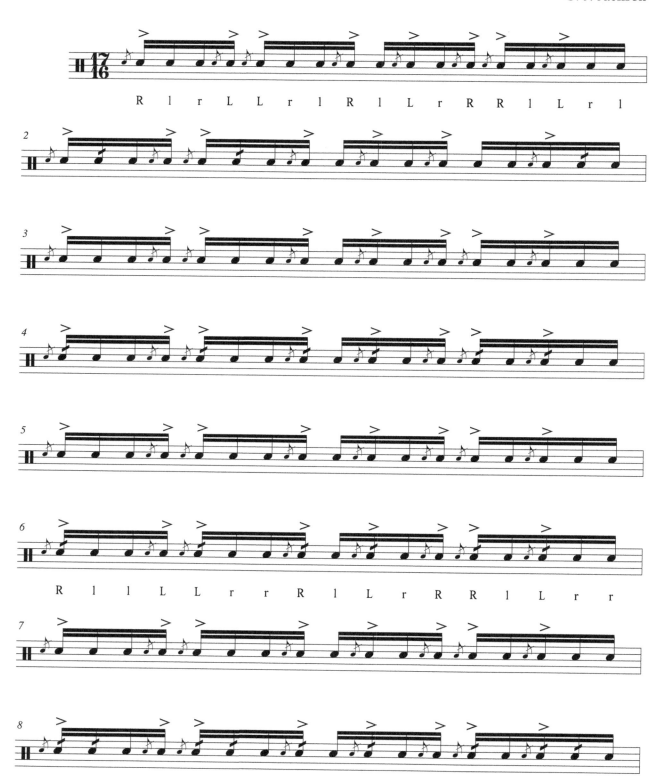

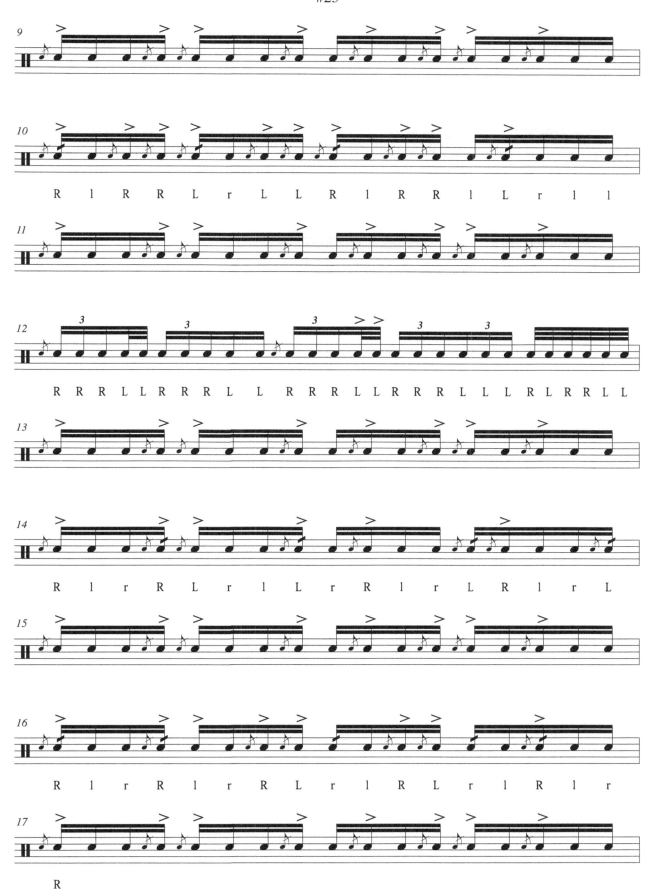

r l l r L   l r r l R   R l   r l r   l r l   L r   l r

l   r l r   l   R r r L R r r L R

#24

G. J. Jackson

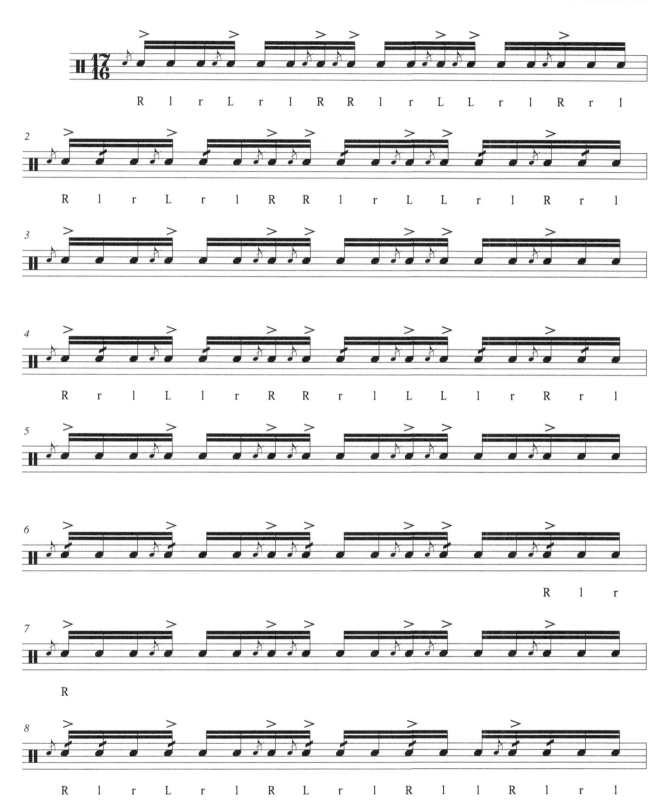

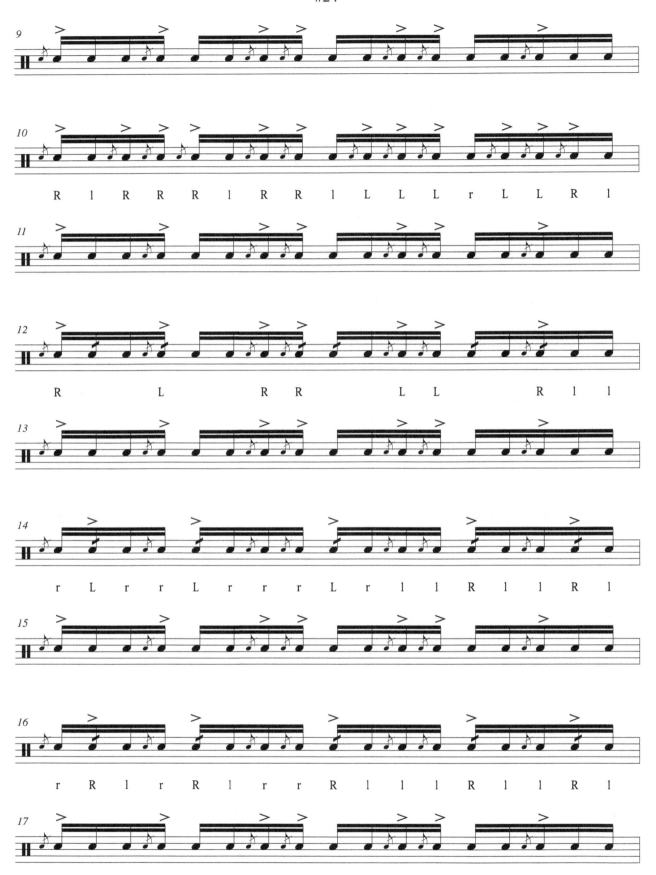

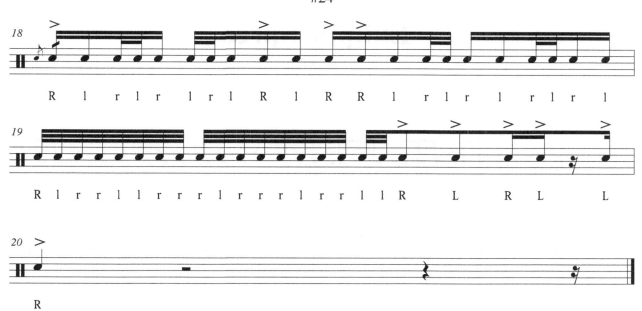

Ekliptic Spree
#25

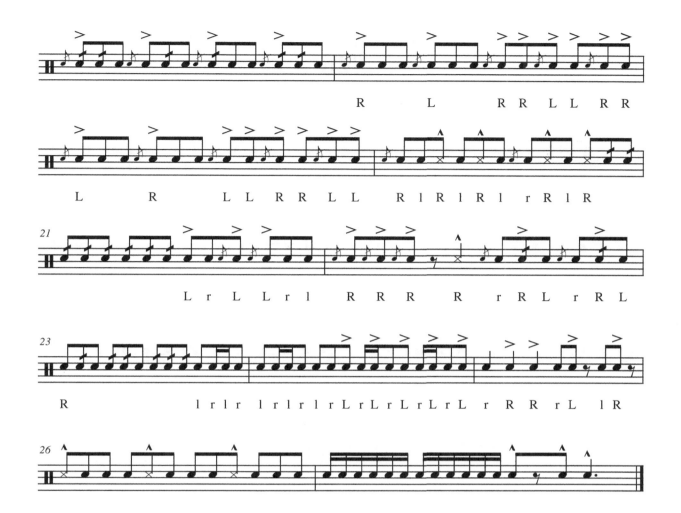

Ekliptic Spree (Remix)
#26

Rapture shopping spree
#27

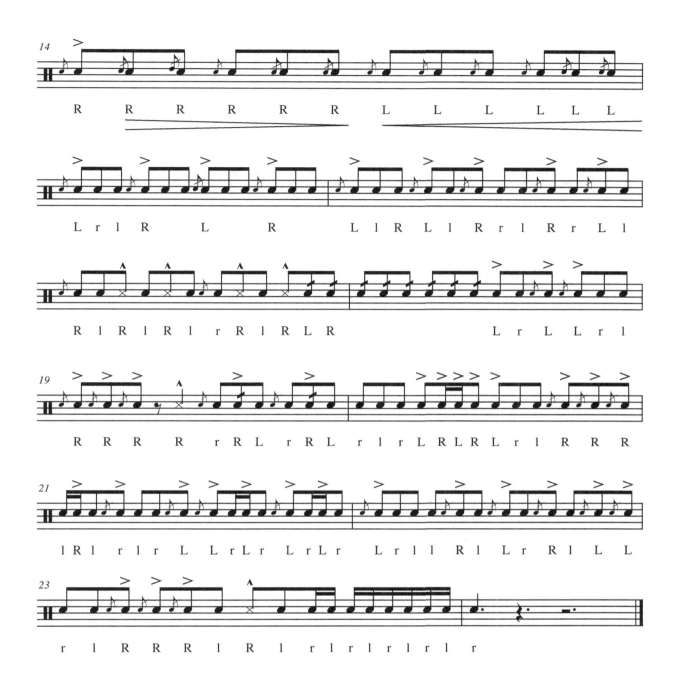

Rapture shopping spree (remix)
#28

Bama Spree 2K2
#29

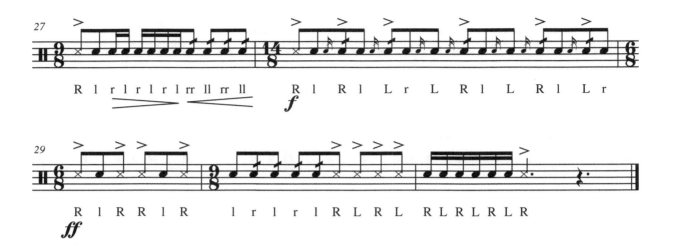

Bama Spree 2K14
#30

64

Ramm

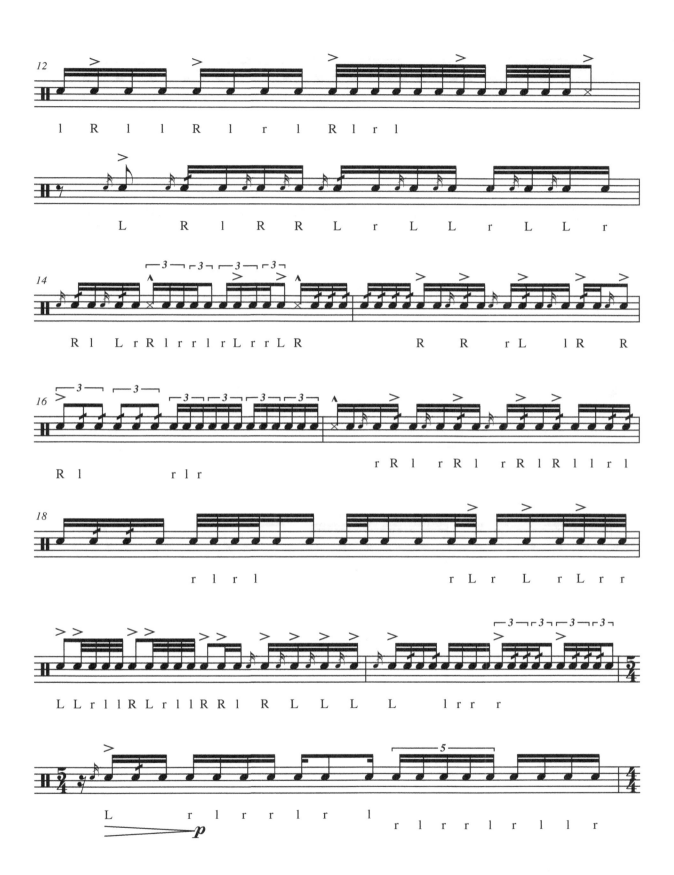

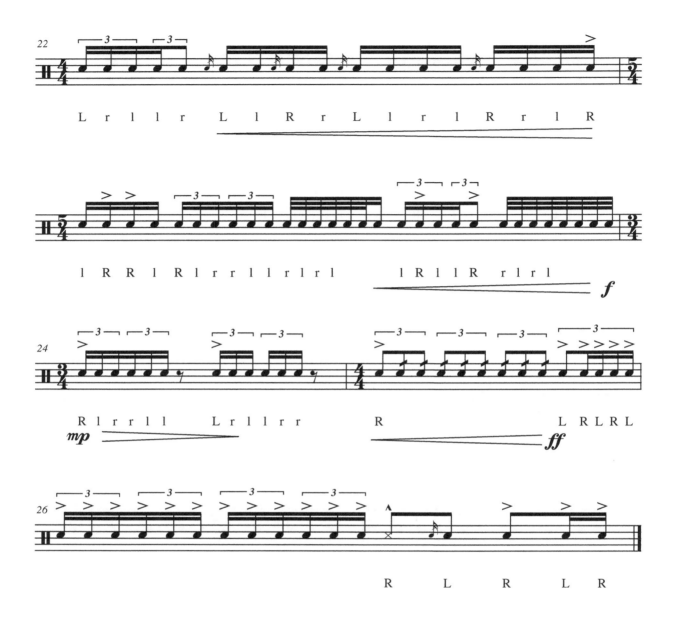

Rapture Online

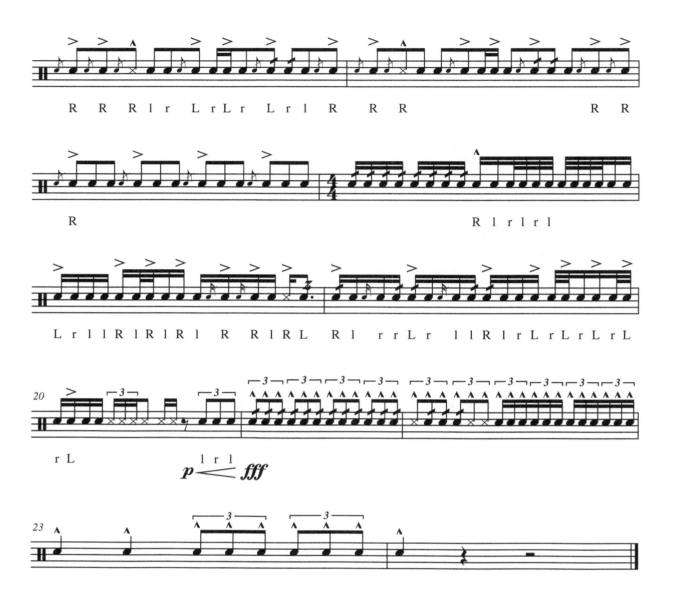

Fearless

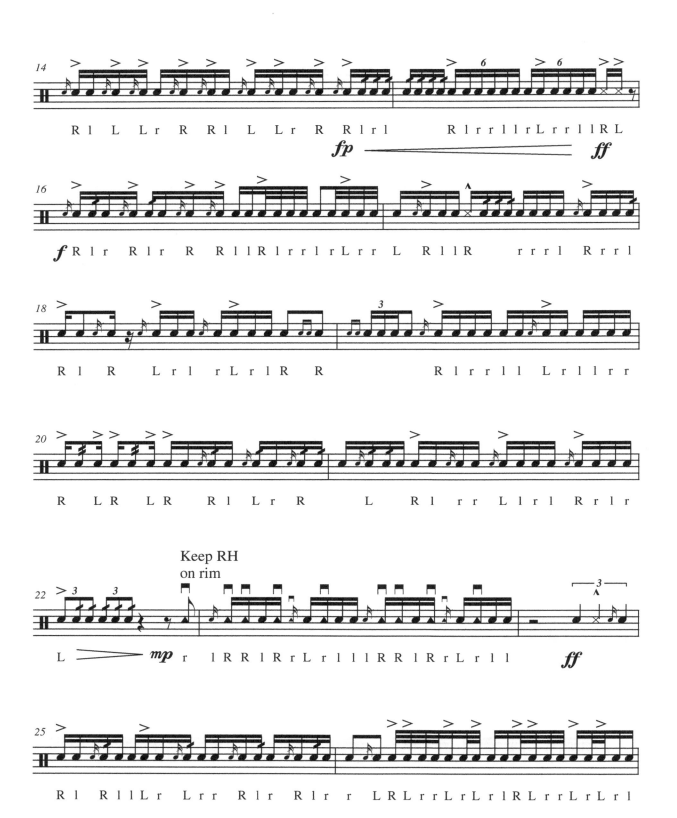

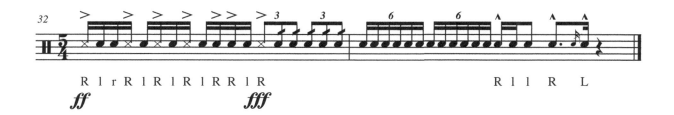

CPSIA information can be obtained at www.ICGtesting.com
Printed in the USA
LVOW02s0055060515

437343LV00020B/109/P

9 781499 188547